I0817217

Fire Station
NEVER MISSED A PERFORMANCE
54
54
F.D.
Heather DiLorenzo Williams
and Warren Rylands
EYEDISCOVER

Go to **www.eyediscover.com** and enter this book's unique code.

BOOK CODE

AVA56732

EYEDISCOVER brings you optic readalongs that support active learning.

Published by AV² by Weigl
350 5th Avenue, 59th Floor New York, NY 10118
Website: www.eyediscover.com

Library of Congress Control Number: 2018953509

ISBN 978-1-4896-8013-6 (hardcover)

Printed in the United States of America
in Brainerd, Minnesota
1 2 3 4 5 6 7 8 9 0 22 21 20 19 18

082018
120917

Project Coordinator: John Willis
Designer: Mandy Christiansen

Weigl acknowledges Alamy, Getty Images, iStock, and Shutterstock as the primary image suppliers for this title.

EYEDISCOVER provides enriched content, optimized for tablet use, that supplements and complements this book. EYEDISCOVER books strive to create inspired learning and engage young minds in a total learning experience.

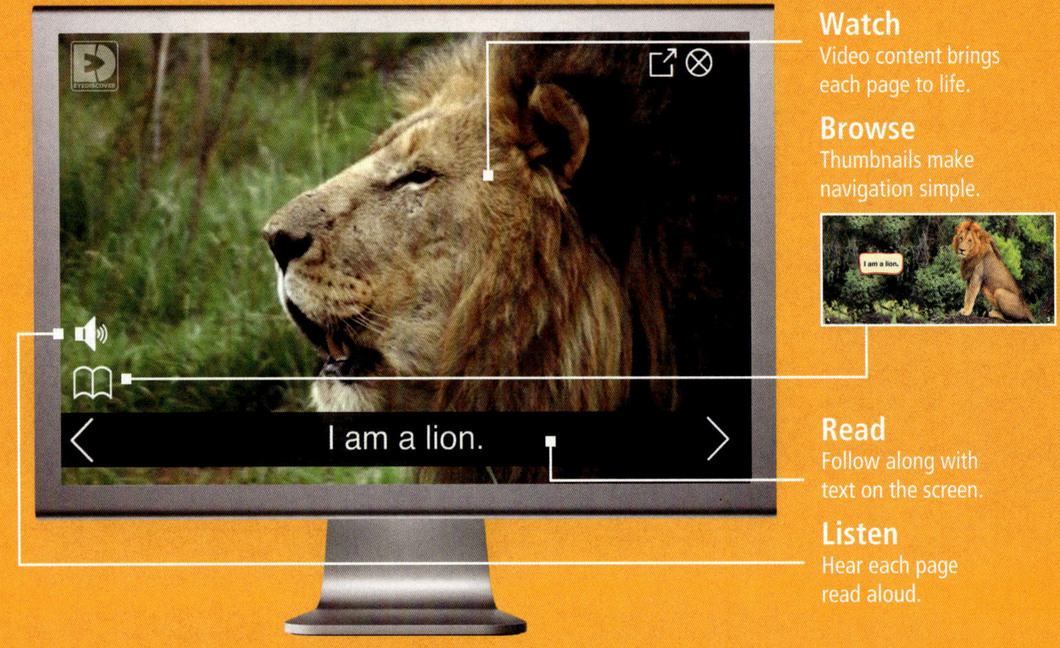

Your EYEDISCOVER Optic Readalongs come alive with...

Audio
Listen to the entire book read aloud.

Video
High resolution videos turn each spread into an optic readalong.

OPTIMIZED FOR

- TABLETS
- WHITEBOARDS
- COMPUTERS
- AND MUCH MORE!

Fire Station

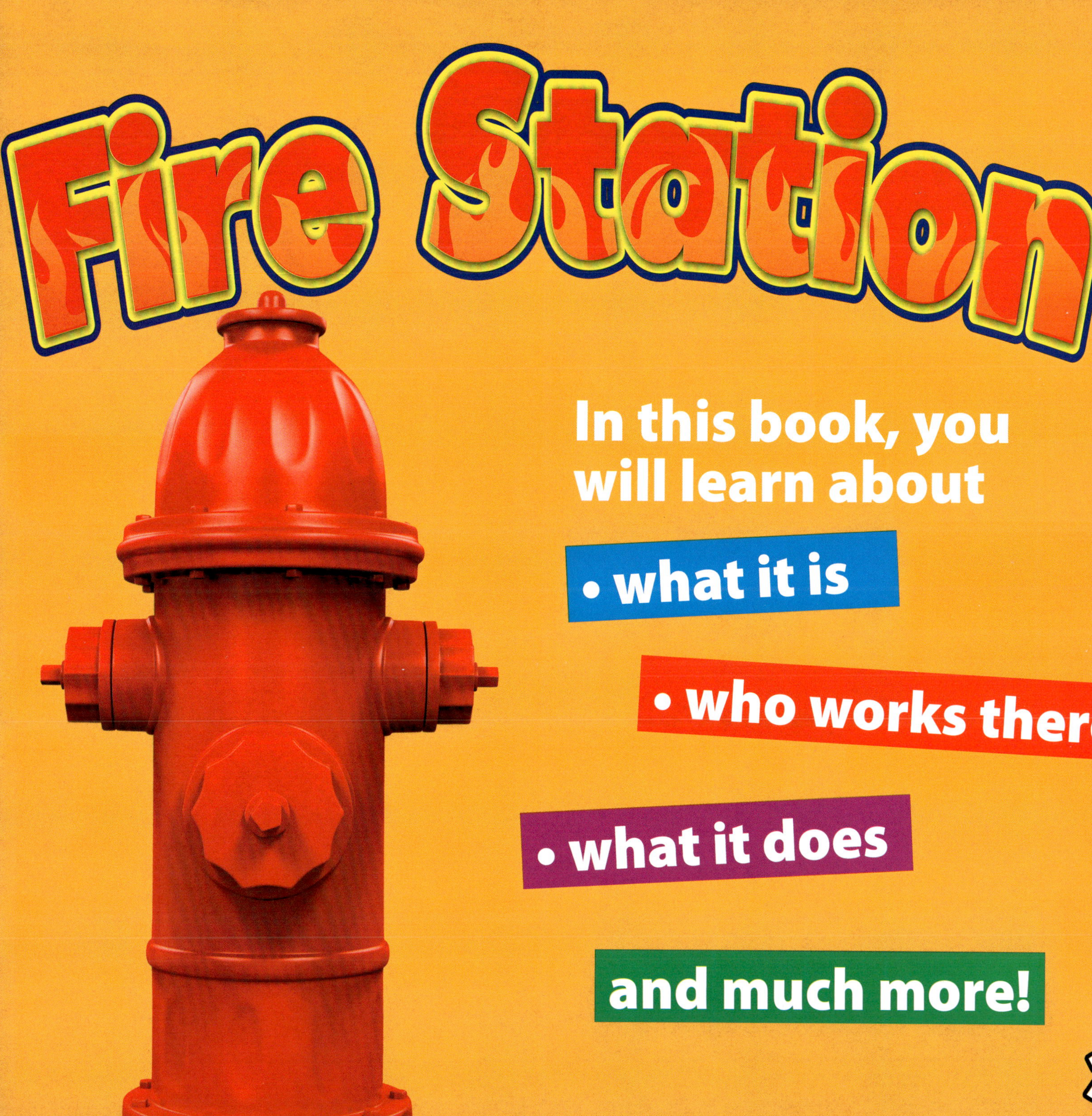

In this book, you will learn about

- what it is
- who works there
- what it does

and much more!

WELLINGTON
319
FIRE
NO PARKING FIRE STATION

A fire station is a building where firefighters work.

SPARTAN
4

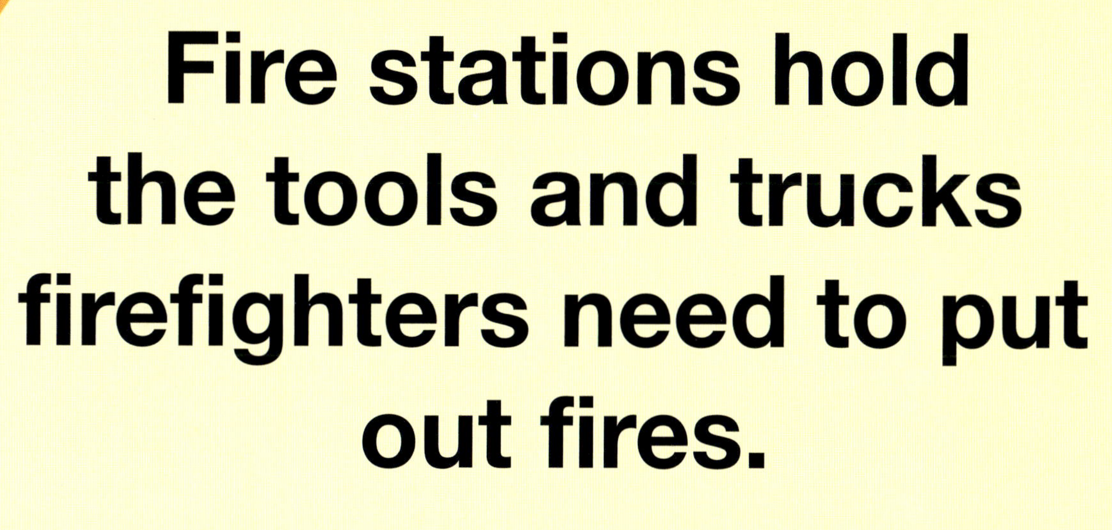

Fire stations hold the tools and trucks firefighters need to put out fires.

Fire trucks are usually red and have a loud siren.

SAN FRANCISCO
AERIAL TRUCK CO.
F.D.
2
FDNY
IN MEMORY

TOWER 1
HAMTRAMCK
FOREST ISLAND
Recycling, Inc.
4837

Fire trucks have ladders to reach high places. They also have long hoses that firefighters can use.

Firefighters also have gear that they wear when fighting fires. This gear keeps firefighters safe during a fire.

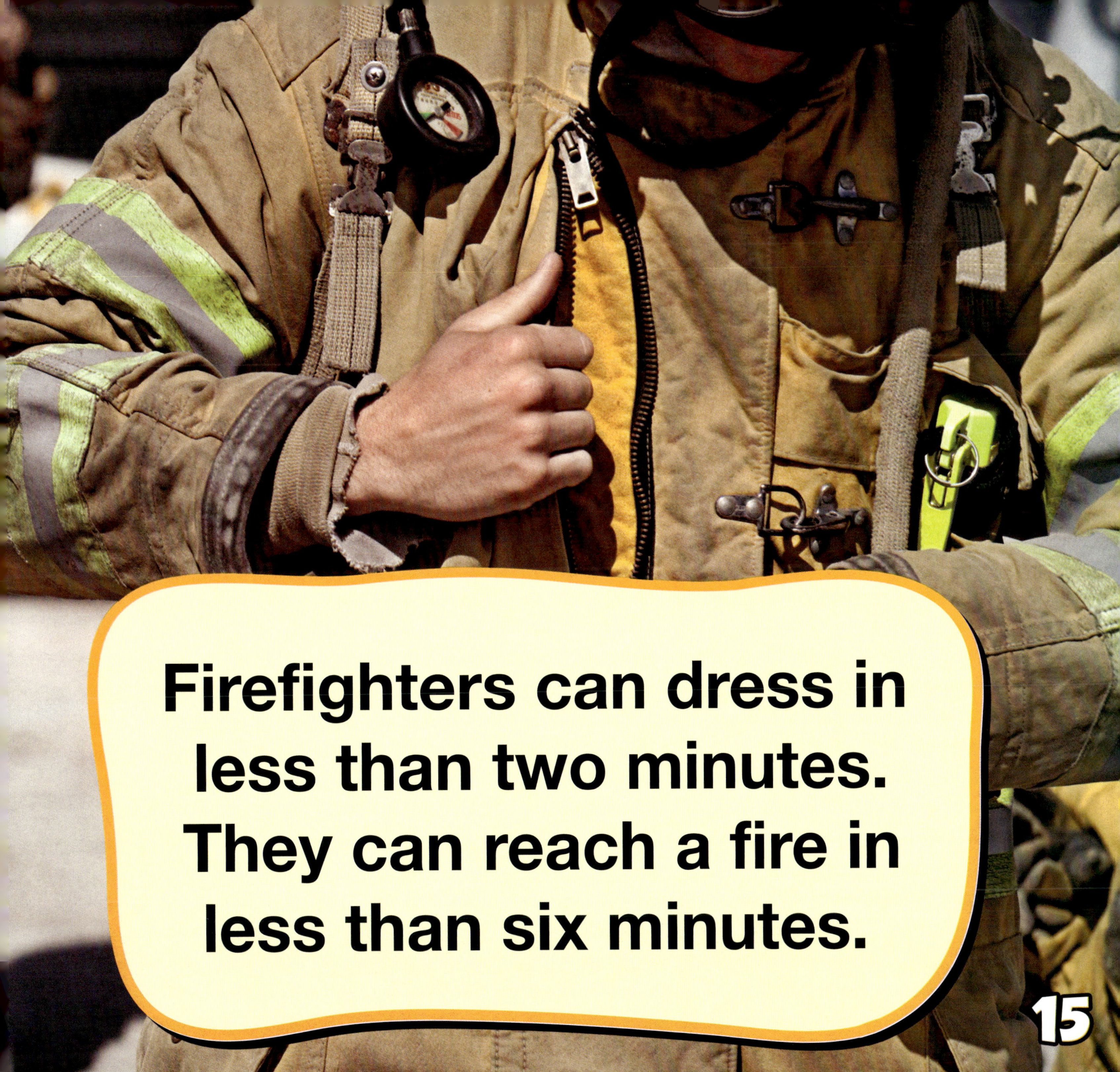

Firefighters can dress in less than two minutes. They can reach a fire in less than six minutes.

Firefighters are called first responders. Sometimes they help people who have been in car crashes.

FIRE
DEPT.
2750

If you
catch fire:
Drop and
roll.

Students can take a class trip to a fire station to learn about fire safety.

Firefighters are real-life heroes. They put themselves in danger to save other people's lives.

FIRE STATION BY THE NUMBERS

There are more than **1 million** fires in **America** each year.

There are more than **1,100,000** firefighters in the **United States.**

There are about **58,750** fire stations In the **United States.**

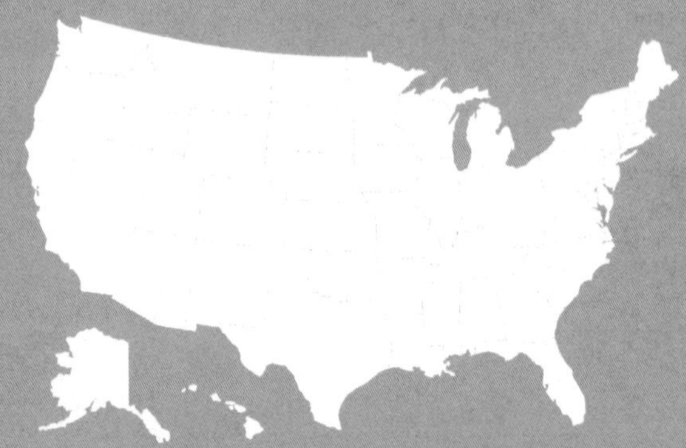

Pennsylvania has **more** fire departments than any other state.

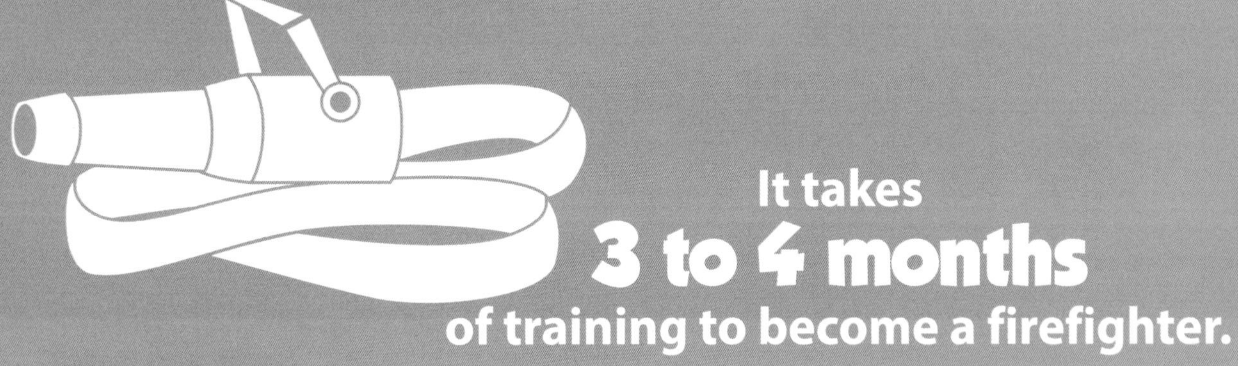

It takes **3 to 4 months** of training to become a firefighter.

An average **fire truck** is **32 feet** long.
(9.75 meters)

KEY WORDS

Research has shown that as much as 65 percent of all written material published in English is made up of 300 words. These 300 words cannot be taught using pictures or learned by sounding them out. They must be recognized by sight. This book contains 36 common sight words to help young readers improve their reading fluency and comprehension. This book also teaches young readers several important content words, such as proper nouns. These words are paired with pictures to aid in learning and improve understanding.

Page	Sight Words First Appearance
5	a, is, where, work
7	and, need, out, put, the, to
8	are, have
11	also, can, high, long, that, they, use
12	this, when
15	in, than, two
16	been, car, first, help, people, sometimes, who
19	about, learn, take
20	life, other

Page	Content Words First Appearance
5	fire, firefighters, station
7	tools, trucks
8	red, siren
11	hoses, ladders
12	gear
16	responders
19	class safety, students
20	heroes

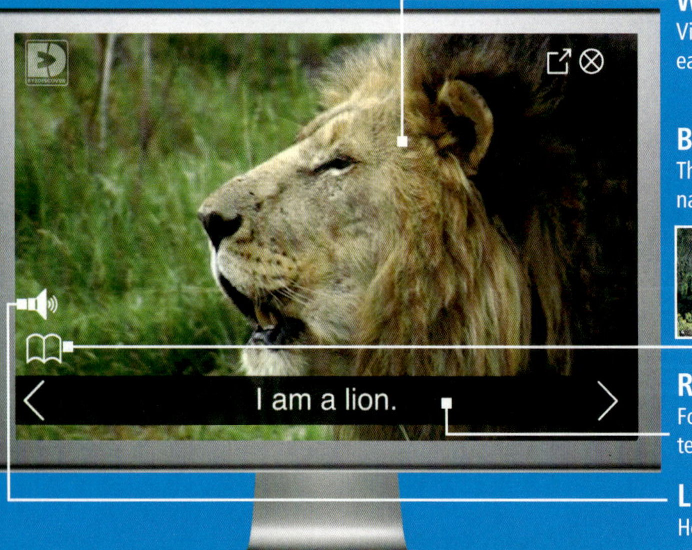

Watch
Video content brings each page to life.

Browse
Thumbnails make navigation simple.

Read
Follow along with text on the screen.

Listen
Hear each page read aloud.

Go to www.eyediscover.com and enter this book's unique code.

BOOK CODE

AVA56732